Paradise

(point of transmission)

Andrew Sutherland is a Queer Poz (PLHIV) writer and performance-maker between Boorloo (Perth, Western Australia) and Singapore. His poetry, fiction and creative non-fiction can be found in a range of publications, including Australian Poetry's B*est of Australian Poems 2021*, *Overland*, *Westerly*, *Cordite*, *Portside Review*, *Running Dog*, Margaret River Press' *We'll Stand in That Place*, and *EXHALE: an anthology of Queer voices from Singapore* (Math Paper Press). He holds a BA (First Class Hons.) of Acting from LASALLE College of the Arts, and in the performance space his credits as a playwright, director, collaborative maker, dramaturg, actor, and arts educator include a myriad of projects with Squid Vicious Theatre, Intercultural Theatre Institute, Renegade Productions, The Esplanade Singapore, Pink Gajah Theatre, and Black Swan State Theatre Company of WA, among others. *Paradise (point of transmission)* is his debut poetry collection. He is grateful to reside on Whadjuk Noongar Bibbulmun land.

Paradise

(point of transmission)

ANDREW SUTHERLAND

FREMANTLE PRESS

'Like ghosts, what inhabits us is neither unequivocally dead nor alive. [...] Since it comes from the otherness of the unconscious, which itself persists atemporally [...] the enigmatic message functions similarly to the virus, since HIV persists beyond the life of its original host.'

Tim Dean, "Bareback Time".

'Squash it into almost nothingness,
into something so small, smaller
than it already is, so it won't show,
cannot be counted,
like ghosts and gases, its true existence
undiscovered, lurking'

Justin Chin, "Undetectable".

contents

(paradise)

About the poems

At the end of 2014, after living, studying, and working in Singapore – my place of chosen residence – through my late teens and early twenties, I was diagnosed HIV-positive. The laws in Singapore forbade HIV-positive foreigners from holding extended residence in Singapore. At the time of diagnosis, we were not even allowed to enter the country as tourists, although that has since been lifted to allow HIV-positive foreigners to travel within the ninety-day tourist window.

I did not immediately leave. The next six months were months of liminal space and borrowed time, as I began antiretroviral treatment in Australia and clung to the fading trace of my life in Singapore, wrapping up arts projects and relationships until finally I was faced with no choice but to accept that my future was in Australia, where I could legally reside and seek treatment. There had always been deep ambivalences and complexities in being a white Australian in the post-colonial, Chinese-Singaporean majority city-state, and HIV transmission meant that the possibility of a hybrid identity was to become something more akin to a dismembered one.

To be diagnosed HIV-positive at this time – as in, perhaps, any time – also represented a liminal kind of space. Well after the 'Lazarus moment' of antiretroviral treatment, but just before the popular or accessible advent of PrEP, it took years for me to decipher how I was to relate to my HIV diagnosis, especially as it was the cause of such a literal upheaval in my residence and sense of self. These poems, primarily written between 2017 and 2021, find themselves within that sequence of physical and psychic journeys: from seronegative to seropositive; from 'growing up' as a resident of Singapore to finding my place as an adult in the Perth of my childhood; as well as from secretive about my HIV-status, in which the art I produced was rooted in the trauma of HIV transmission without naming it, towards a more public life. These poems creep around what scholar Tim Dean, who writes with great clarity about the complex shadows surrounding contemporary HIV transmission, would describe as a kind of haunting.

In (*narrative*), transmission and diagnosis are written as moments of rupture: of sacrifice or violence, of movement and of break. Histories and mythologies, both personal and observed, are recast over the spectre of seroconversion. In (*metaphor*), the poems track the movement between spaces, tracing the shadows of residence, citizenship and the self in the gap between Singapore and Perth. Finally, in (*paradise*), these concerns coalesce into a different set of hauntings: attempts toward new signifiers and new mythologies, in which continuous or persistent living-with-HIV is characterised by Queer modalities of intimacy, yearning and transformation.

Almost all of these poems were written on Whadjuk Noongar Bibbulmun land, and the publisher of this book stands on Walyalup. I wish to acknowledge the traditional custodians of the land on which I reside and the long, unbroken line of stories told by First Nations peoples in so-called Australia. I acknowledge that sovereignty of this land was never ceded, and I pay my respects to elders past and ongoing.

I also wish to acknowledge the privilege that has allowed me to write this book and to live a public life as an HIV-positive individual. It is not something that was easy to do, and I do not take the privilege lightly. Everyone's relationship to disclosure with HIV must be their own. This includes the privileges and protections that my ethnicity, nationality, gender identity, as well as the class and familial structures around me, afford me in this country.

If you have purchased this book, you might consider providing financial support or mutual aid to the lived experience of Poz communities, in particular by paying the rent to Queer and/or HIV+ First Nations peoples through organisations like BlaQ, or in assistance of HIV+ migrants through organisations like the HIV/AIDS Legal Centre. I strongly encourage you to research ways you can best provide support or reach out to your local or regional HIV/AIDS peak body or peer-led organisation.

(narrative)

AIDS Play 1991

This is the year I was born.

Re-creation. Context & its dizzy cries.
Whenever we choose memory, it lives only
for the sake of those who are yet waiting.

If I had to identify death, it would be as the cat
under the wheel of some childhood neighbour's car.
After that, it's just another thought about a road.

I don't think I can be responsible for describing loss.

Virgo '91. In this scene, I'm Time.
In this scene, Time represents a baby.
Interested actors perform the past, & I

cry at all the wrong moments. The past
performs a sickness. Time is still a baby.
The Reaper turns four on TV. 1991,

2014, 2021: I want to write a history
that speaks precious little. How I keep
my mornings swallowed: 2021, 2014, 1991.

As a newborn in 1991, I have no knowledge of or connection to the
AIDS crisis, except one sharp & unexpected burst of memory,
in which I recalled my HIV diagnosis back in 2014 –

World Tree

for Edith Podesta

(Robertson Quay, Singapore)

The day I tested positive, I walked from the clinic at the quay to my old university. And, I am sorry to admit, as I walked through the city – a forest built to scrape the sky – I pictured myself at the top of each tower. A lean. A glance. A wobble. Still, I continued to walk. Each building became a tree, or the branch of a tree, fused together from a fire and asking permission to be fire, again. I looked up, and with the daylight's sun, I thought I could make out the moon and stars.

And I heard the bark of dogs.

The sun and the moon started to shake, vibrating with terror, and I saw a pack of hounds, drooling and baying, dashing across the blue sky. The sun and the moon tried to flee across the heavens, but the hounds could not be outrun. All the burning trees from which I longed to fall shuddered around me as the sun and the moon were snuffed out; torn apart by the gaping jaws of dogs. And slowly, one by one –

the stars started to drop from the sky like flies.

They fell out of sight, and as they fell, sight too fell away – and all that remained for me to see was an image of myself suspended upon the last light of a sky-scraping branch, like an outdated magazine in a waiting room, or the tiniest drop of blood on a thumb. Hanging from the tree, eye torn from a socket's grasp, dripping vision down the path below.

Yet still, I continued to walk.

Because that will not be me. Every day I keep my two eyes widened, clutched like lanterns; beaming from my skull, and brightening, too. I climb branches only to confirm the leaves, and the baying sounds of dogs don't follow.

137 near Trujillo

137 sets.   Chan Chan to Las Llamas.
And just dug up, in greatest numbers
found – remains – and of a sole event.

Yes, all at once, a single march, just
one event   perhaps a time of crisis,
a particularly special need   to leave
a legacy behind, largest in the world
so far   and maybe I'll suggest
for now / for now / still now   –   we
know this as the cradle of mankind.

Lesions to the breastbone, dislocated
ribs; a cut, a move, remove. 137 sets
of little sternums   skulls   the many fragile
bones of feet   with toes to march
together   Chan Chan to Las Llamas.

Perhaps a time of crisis   the stormy
weather needing answer   yes   all at
once   largest known offering of its
type   the scale is incredible   all in
the past   uniquely fascinating habit
of a civilisation, of a time, though I'll
admit   at times I've had the thought
we're tucked within our cradle, still?

200 camelids, too – in choral screams
from other throats to join with 137:
as still there's need for every set of
hands held   jaws gaping   knees buckled
by the weight of all they are to give

        and there must be something
we can do about the weather –

And I wonder if it's worth
remembering: beasts of
burden face the mountains

all children face the sea.

Loop

when street cats
stare snake-eyed
and each snake carries
a cat's-eye

when pot plants
only starve
or drown; and
even the dishwasher
looks super disappointed

when you put your fucking headphones on.

when the past
keeps breaking
its commitment;
perpetual resurrector,
these flowers
from a nec-
romantic heart

though the original is always chosen
over the re-make. and even now
I suspect I might be one of the
violent men, after all.

when the cum
is dopamine,
escaping

when paradise is desire
or disgust, and it never
mattered which

when you tell a person how they are mistaken,
before they ever find the words to speak.

tell me what I don't know.
I'm waiting for you to say when.

Sodom & Gomorrah

we throw these names around
like any old thing
a city as behaviour as a lifestyle
history / a future / doom

actually, my friend told me
the people of Sodom & Gomorrah were erased
because they ravished angels
I was going to google but then got bored
& decided to just roll with it

& oh! those tantalising halos
that we may know
the perfect length of wing
they could almost be swans but fuckable

heaven as a host of fuckable swans, each hissing for oblivion
is this divine? look not behind
be blind be pillars of salt
be bare-backed nations such strange flesh

sin is probably a failure of the imagination
we do so often hurt people, though
sometimes I think I'd like to see myself vanish
if only for a little while?

maybe after douching

sure I think sodomy's great
but I don't think I've ever tried gomorry??
... is a joke I should probably cut from this poem
... is a question that doesn't ever keep me up at night

& I'm not saying I'm an angel, but –
would it be so surprising if I were to wake in feathers?

I really got into cinema around the same time I fell into sex
& in a bleaker orgy had the clarity of mind
to lean back & quote *Salò* to the fuck-thick air
the reference was lost on all involved
but I still laughed & kept at it

this part's just to let you know, this is not a sex-negative poem
& just to let you know (as far as I know)
no angels were harmed while writing
& also FYI I'm into suffering, not pity
unless later I want something from you
in which case, salt-pity will have to do

I want my fucking to be rough & oh so languid
like it was in the old days
those days of being wild
those halcyon genesis days

I want to try sodgorrah
just you & I: gomodom
I know that sounds like another joke but it belongs here anyway
I am deep & copious; well-watered & green
fuck me like twin cities
fuck me like utopia's coming
it's coming

actually, the only names that still interest me from the Bible
are Salome & Judith
& isn't that funny??
how it all comes to a head

Salome

for Stefanos Rassios

A poster for a production of the Strauss opera catches my eye, and on a whim I message Stefanos. *Random question, but why haven't you ever directed a* Salome? *It seems right up your alley.* The sex and blood; the beheading. The lurid, lesser passion play of it all. *I suppose it's never caught my attention,* he answers. *Why? Are you thinking of doing one?* No, but the possibility of *Salome* has been on my mind, of late. Maybe I would play the lead. // Seroconversion is the time period in which HIV antibodies develop and become detectable in the blood. The body's efforts to defend itself against the virus inevitably fail. The immune system becomes compromised, and it is no longer your body, entirely – it is now your body + HIV. You are likely to experience an intense bout of fatigue, fever, and ache, as your cells rehearse the multiplication – the movement – that will be performed from here into the future. Once this internal choreography has been learnt, the outer shell of sickness will pass. Afterwards, you will test positive. // *It's tricky to find anything sympathetic about Salome,* Stefanos texts. I admit I hadn't given much thought to character. *Bring me the head of John the Baptist,* she says. Not a selfish demand, but the only plausible recompense for unchecked ability. What else could be enough? Salome's talent curves with exponential growth, which might itself be the opposite of sympathy. A performance, in exchange for the head of a prophet. // When I experienced seroconversion, I was rehearsing a shadow dance for a corporate entertainment gig. Behind a screen, the outline of my body was supposed to approximate a lion's head, then seamlessly shift shape as the dance unfolded. For two weeks, I felt I was more sickness than body. Drowning in impossible weakness, I would crawl into pitiful lion shape, desperate only to move. Did I pray to God? Why is it that I can't remember? On the other side of the screen: the head of a lion, before the shadow transforms again. // Does this mean that when Salome dances, she is dancing the death of prediction? Put another way, Salome dances the sheerness of the present. Which means that even after the event – when everything is over – Salome is still dancing. Salome dances, with the ceaseless multiplication of the present. Now Salome continues to dance.

Breed

i. wet

it's very long
big, big, life's
so long – and
your pythonic
yearnings *take your unwrapping*
basic needs
no thing be-
tween; care-
less by design

yes squeeze
that growing
length and *fling me far beyond*
what I was
taught, what
un-fun brains
no longer care

yes: that growing length.
okay: take your unwrapping.
still: to fling me far beyond.

and as they
evaporated
into thin air
it's like no-
body else
was angry and if
they were what
did it matter
no malice

parts of machines
that could no
longer run – they
pulled away just
pull away not out
but flinging far
in slow, slow
motion; vacuum
it was always
meant to be

and you: you're
kindling, you,
you represent
(yes you're
a sign) all
things that could
be set ablaze,
but wet, so
purely wet,
damp centring
like a universe
of orbits, nothing
orbiting, like
cruelty, praying
for a world rammed
back and forth
the axes; I'm
the centre *spilling*

ii. whimper

each cold and new desire
is first made of a mouth
that never can be filled.

not completely. always
there is room for more.
you'd better drop your jaw.

but I'm a talker: beg, narrate.
paw feebly at the door
just half a step behind,

still waiting to roll over.
a bad actor, though I love
to play a role. and as a whole

damp declarations voiced in
pants and pitches from some
other world are barely worth

a variation. hunger is
a solo-cycle, written for
a choir. words spent for you

alone repeat into a rumbling
moan, a bound-mouthed thunder;
forever calling for the next.

my lips speak muzzles, little licks,
but wolf grins have no sound,
unless you hear a scraping

of the teeth. don't I deserve
my whimpers be believed?
these open jaws I've wettened

are to prepare you for
what's yours – inside of me.
I like to think I'm sure I feel

a howling; you bury yourself deep.

iii. waste

there is a long shadow.
there, with aftermath.
this is what lives
at the core of the earth.
at the root. in every branch.

a doubling. a splitting.
there is a half and half.
there, with afterimage.
what grows of memories
near the surface of the soil.

time is a two-way street. this is a closing door.

to be shaped by all the bodies
held before you. to be shaped to
all the bodies that await an after.
drag make-up in your housemate's bed.
I need time to kiss me back.

control yourself. this is certainty.
beloved gods stay where you leave them.
I'm waiting underneath the change.
the future remembers how to leak.

Treatment [3/12/14]

(Sir Charles Gairdner Hospital)

my first with *name* there was
another in the waiting room name
and birthdate *day month year*
I don't know what to make of

twelve
in total arms to cover many
for the measuring for the system
sequencing the likelihood take one
in combination *if I skipped* resist –

this is somewhat troubling.
it can wait returning if need be
give six see three
work my mind
been exercising
I don't expect cold need today
the first person apart from my
parents that I've seen

and even the
doctor said the worst survive
by hiding my ethics open
present *kick the deck* see
how cards fall
too early in relation *if I am to*
spend more time that stops me
in my tracks.

my brief experience.
disappointed I won't be
there to see. Warmest –

Angrboda

her name translates to:

one who brings grief

alternatively –

she who offers sorrow

and lately, I've been having this dream.
I am walking through the streets, but
the buildings are wrecked and deserted.
the city of my dreams in ruin. nobody
walks these paths. nobody lives, or
switches on a light, or laughs, re-builds.

further down the road: no language.

in the next room, soon
it will be New Year's Eve.

and then I can sense something behind
me. following me. I look down at my
feet, and I'm already running. I fall –
and turn to see a great giant looming
above me. she lifts me up – and with
a mask of quiet across her face

she puts me between
her teeth. she breaks
me in two.

her teeth translate to:

I did everything I could

alternatively –

I couldn't protect you

Treatment [20/12/14]

(Sir Charles Gairdner Hospital)

My dearest … you asked me
to greet the passing time
        in the following ways:

Rejection: at breakfast / idea
take a year … treat it as
project management / fall
back … oppressive silence

Hope: despite how it feels
if this doesn't satisfy you
random act of / see you next

Exchange: waiting / handing out flyers for
a Korean church … I accepted gratefully
/ praying to Jesus makes him feel /
'sick or visit?' … both are true
trying to become / he never knew

the carpentry … until after
so happy / in January
I probably won't … but
                the easy-going happiness –

Trickster

I remember the day you turned into a fish. We went down to the river; it was sunny, and so beautiful. You grinned at me and dived into the water, and when you came up you were a fish, darting so fast into the stream. I thought, you always do whatever it is you want. People don't worship that trait the way they ought to. I wanted to jump in after you, but I'd never have kept up, so I cut open my chest, scooped you up and let you swim through my veins. My heart is beating like a river.

Treatment [26/05/15]

(Royal Perth Hospital)

went through / well, I'm still going through
and in November / I'll go back
Easter's hard for me … I recovered
then diagnosed … to jump from
phone calls / hugged me / I *maintained*.
piece of … body … on my mind
and this would have been April.
and April is always a terrible month

to buy a crucifix … now deceased
very dramatically, one of those *signs*.
this balcony / felt so low
I held it up … I said if … owe me
God … it means … to carry … yourself.
I don't know if I ever / I don't know if I
pre-cancerous / touchstone / so much blood
expel … and then *fine* … continue –

um, crazy / and I felt that exhaustion again.
and I say to people … but I *know*.
omnipresent / that's a part of me, too
out of convenience … sacrifice, no altar
you're just giving yourself constantly to yourself
I've wasted my brain and what's still left is
all / you / a person.

to the 14-year-old writing *Buffy the Vampire Slayer* fan fiction

red hair resting on a lover's
shoulder, feet floating high
above the ground; a bullet
through the back, black-eyed
and bleary, each night a little
later, adolescent webbing
threaded through

your screaming dreams, slash
pairings bursting forth, the lonely
heroics of private school, first
kisses, the pale-boy education
you consume.

and still to come, your fresh
held hands, Sarah McLachlan
tears, wide-mouthed stone
men, grasping at swords –

when every lengthening
year your own big bad
is growing; new wars
against your hollow self.

and how many re-runs
does it take to know
oneself? since in time
the hopes you hold
will be less, though perhaps
each one may bear a strength,
an undead heart
of fiction, fighting.

we go camping in the woods with the most derivative witches

I've been thinking of getting into folk horror, which is to say there's not a lot going on in my life. Time made me a body when I could have been a forest or a lake. A collection of stones patterned ominously in the dirt. The blades of grass digesting down a goat. Instead, to be this momentary crawl. Time agrees to be a tunnel & builds itself transparent, on the promise that we won't look past the glass. Horror politely shuts its eyes. Just outside the gate, a parking meter's been ticking for 96 uninterrupted hours, though I only hear it when I'm waiting for the past. Nothing truly unsettles me anymore, except perhaps the word repeat. Still – let this be a symbol. Let me bare my throat to background noise. Pointless metronome, be my Pazuzu. Be my Scandinavia in summer. Time, become a body of horror. Sometimes, in the spaces between blood tests, I fall pregnant with the devil. A touch of genre helps the silences stay Camp. Oh – invisible gestation. Nervous systems rehearse themselves into landscape; before too long, this landscape shall imagine me. Never fall asleep together; anything but that soft cliff-face. Edge a little closer to repeat. In the spaces between blood tests, I birth only sequels. & I've been thinking of getting out of folk horror, but I can't shake the suspicion that the future only intends to be the past, delayed. I once hooked up with a guy who made me wear a crown of leaves while I gave him head, & Netflix didn't even buy the rights. To understand your body by its end scenes is inevitable when romancing a man of sticks. Be deciduous in undressing. Be set ablaze, again. Sit timeless on the sidewalk, & suddenly the ticking stops. Look – I am earthed with desire. Both hands grasp the shaky cam. Veins as petal, petal, petal: the gory climax, ecstatic underneath the skin. The witches' wailing reunion with immunology. Hit record, & time goes dark again. To be the protagonist is to also be the offering. Oh, yes – the long silence still waits.

Budgerigar

i.

couple A and couple B room-share. couple A lay eggs. couple B lay eggs. they keep them warm. when couple A have their backs turned, couple B smash all of couple A's eggs. there is no visible mourning. all of couple B's eggs hatch. there is no visible celebration. shortly after, as their residence is being cleaned, couple B slip past the gates and fly away. they are never seen again. couple A is left to raise couple B's children. there is no visible confusion.

ii.

Open up the cage, and one, two,
seven take their wings into the sky.
No hesitation; no one looking back.
They'll probably all be eaten
by bigger birds, or they won't
know how to feed themselves, but
I'm selfish, I have to go, besides –
they're in the air now, out of mind.
Time to leave the metal wire behind.

One, green and yellow, hits the grass.
It bounces, runs. A malformed wing;
I hadn't noticed. The nameless bird
was never going to fly. Perhaps
he didn't know, until he failed.
And all the other birds had left him
to live on the lawn alone, a frantic
blur of green on green. I chase the bird
around the yard. My foolish hands

catch hold of the terrified bundle;
return him to the cage in which his
broken wings were born. I fill it up
with seed and water; all that I
have left. It will all disappear,
before too long. I'm going soon,
I say. Flightless in a finished home.
But someone will take care of you.
Somebody's got to take care of you.

afterwards, bring me back me as Tom Cruise's wig in *Interview with the Vampire*

I want to wear intimacy
the way a 90s leading man wears a head of curls
with violent ease
the way a gay pre-teen wears Halloween fangs
with troubling sincerity
& it's not that I think I'm not convincing
it's only that I'm not convinced

I want to be a trick of the light
if to be truly intimate with someone
is to no longer be at all yourself
intimacy is not a fancy cape
something you put on, like an American accent at drama school
intimacy is not another Tennessee Williams scene study
it is not finally being allowed to play Blanche
although if it were a cape, oh boy would I wear it
I would vanish with the becoming of it all

I want to trickle down a neck
like it's cinematic feeding time
& the soundtrack knows to swell for necks
make my own cells swoon
with barely a pump of the heart
how each would fall into the other!
to be shadowed by grand pianos
I want to eat Christian Slater

I want to one day look at myself
the way an alligator looks at the Eiffel Tower
with an honest-to-fucking-god tear in its eye
because the Eiffel Tower's just a stack of alligators
& what's an alligator if not a hungry Eiffel Tower??

I want to be stripped clean of it all
naked & approximately true, adorned with just the necessary pieces
god, I'd be so real!
or maybe I could be the costume
yes, I'd like to be the costume –

I once said to a particularly buttoned-up boyfriend that
Interview with the Vampire was the best mainstream AIDS film of the '90s
& I think it finally pushed him over the edge
he was the type to bring up the virus every time we had sex
without necessarily realising he was doing it
sometimes I would joke about it, like:
guess we'd better tell that condom it needs to get tested
& sometimes I would just smile quietly & remember

isn't it about vampires? he had snapped
there'd already been a bruising chat about postmodern art
why can't you just let things be about what they're about?
you think it makes you sound so smart, but honestly – you are impossible
just let me have this, I thought
Tom Hanks in *Philadelphia* didn't get to raise a precocious Kirsten Dunst
Tom Hanks in *Philadelphia* mostly had to die??
yes, I want to be impossible
impossible curls & intimate with every cell
bedecked with something new
so let me have this

I watch the student actors perform *Angels in America* the day after I am diagnosed positive

at transmission, I don't know where I am
at intermission, Edith tells me I should go
afterwards, I say it wasn't the sickness
    it was when the angel said, *stop moving* –
that's the part I couldn't bear to hear

my housemate sobs when I call her, though not for me
    an uncle who had died when she was a child
perhaps she cries the way I cried for Paddy Chew:
        archive footage only
    I want to scream, *Hannah – history's not here*

looking back, I fear there's nothing here.

deface my year-old headshots; scrawl *let me in* in dripping gold
lead the warm-up, though my vital parts stay cool
    I could never nail a monologue the way you do
don't you think seeing a 20-year-old in stage makeup sarcoma is hideous?
    & somehow, so banal

remember how, barely 19, that first-semester movement coach
    told me I danced like an angel? how I thanked her
  till she slapped my legs; said *no, you're playing goblin*
        now, you move like goblin

right – I can hardly remember it, either.

I never thought I'd say it, kids,
    but I'm tired of queering history
  isn't it funny, how we walk the tightrope of time?
when years from now, my name will tread no list

you pull the cart across the desert
all the way to Rochor
God only descends in rope
I could be in Shanghai dancing Xiqu
but I'll never get a visa now

oh, my children, I'm sorry I still think of you as mine.

department heads will crumble
institutions were designed to fail you
narrative will fail you
to act, at all, will fail you

the student angel cries, *stop moving* –
the diction of it strains against the walls.

Narrative

On a first date, he tells me about his job. They keep mice. The mice are tested, experimented on, lab rats but mice. Some are made sick and perhaps some are healed. The males and the females are kept separate. He tells me about a boy-mouse and a girl-mouse that he liked. They looked so cute together, those two little mice. He daydreamed about them, and one day, by accident or by waking dream, left them in the same cage. Some time later, his superiors came to him to tell him that a female mouse was pregnant. They knew it was his fault – his job was on the line – and nothing could be born. That same day he killed the pregnant mouse. He tells me that afterwards, he looked for the boy-mouse in its enclosure but could no longer distinguish him from the other males. I take him home – perhaps we were already home? – and kiss him, rough. I close his rapid heart beneath my grip; wonder why it is that I so yearn to feel the shared pulse of mammals. Years later, I remember the way the mice needed one another. How they learnt the language just to tell him, *let us love each other and die*. How he spent a shallow breath to tell me, *I would risk certainty just for a chance with you*. I don't remember his name. We were never given any of their names.

(metaphor)

Metaphor

I ask Wan Ching how she is. *Are you lonely? At home on whatever-floor.* She replies, *I have had mysterious droppings on my floor for some time.* Her brother-in-law sends pictures to a biologist friend. Apparently, the droppings of a bat. *Never seen the animal,* Wan Ching writes. *Just been cleaning up its mess.* Log on HDB feng shui forums: wi-fi geomancers tell us, *time to buy 4D.* We know we're lucky upside-down. In sleep I never dream of wings, but flap into the night the same; depending on the angle. Actually – isn't a bat technically always the right side up? For what it needs to do, I mean. *I'm not a gambling person,* but one of my worst fears is being a vector, and never realising what I've done. An essay on viral dramaturgy lurks in my browser history, though I'm not sure if I ever plan to read it. *I'm a scientific person, too.* No one ate the bat; *just happen to fly by.* Echolocation doesn't work if nothing's there in front of you. *I don't compare advice*; no point wondering what to think. *I just enjoy the luck* – and not so lonely, either. Wan Ching's yet to see her guest. Finally, I type: d*o you think maybe the bat is a metaphor?* She says, *the bat might be, but the shit is real.*

ghosts should walk on clean stages

& every August I run a little sweep –
though my papers never burn; they're getting damp
beneath a thumbprint & a stamp. I still inhale the ash,
& tramp the smoky east-side streets to watch pale actors
scream ancestors we forgot to dream.   & I remain

in memories of smaller shrines, the way I never
appreciated seventh-month streets till I was finally
made to leave, as per the time the shades accepted
that it could have been the cats to scratch my arms
like that; the skyped-in tears, the days I overslept
through last farewells – though who will blame me

when an airport's just a temple for the swallowing
of hungrier half-men; & each sidewalk is a tarmac
temple, too. & have you ever walked upon a stage
that didn't crease the dirt into your protoplasmic
heels? how easily I win beliefs at once: un-
known, mis-made, un-own; in a clean sweep.

Guanyin

i.

Some days past my return, I notice for the first time that atop a corner bookshelf in my parents' apartment sits a ceramic statue of Guanyin. When had she arrived? Had she preceded me home, or had she appeared while I was sleeping? I finally ask my mother. *We picked her up visiting you in Singapore. On the street with all the temples. I don't know who she is, but I thought she looked beautiful.* She's the Goddess of Mercy, I tell my mother. I say it's a very touristy thing to do; but I suppose everything is when you're a tourist. I feel a deep unrest to see her there: this goddess that does not belong to us, and all the mercies we can never account for. Still, there is something imposing about Guanyin sitting up there: assured and stable upon an otherwise mediocre shelf. The weight of her. I see myself taking apart all the shelving stacked in every home I've lived; all beneath Guanyin.   When I move, I bring her with me. My housemate, years away from Taiwan, calls her Ma; speaks to her when wi-fi fails. My boyfriend, who never knew his mother, doesn't cast his eyes over Guanyin at all. Picture her in each residence I might still be living in. The apartment with the party princess; the crowded Chinatown HDB; the ninth floor with the nosy landlord; the white house on East Coast Road. Each day, a little closer to the ocean. A sculpture is not a visa. Time spent is not belonging. Let me be a tourist to myself. Imagine Guanyin there: in pasts now begging to commence.

ii.

Guanyin does not face out of the window.
I'd rather she not be looking at the sea; or maybe
the horizon. I keep her turned toward the kitchen.

Kettle: Trash.

Microwave: Trash.

Oven: Never use.

May as well
not be there.

IKEA sets, matching plates; all that sprawling
mass – non-descriptors bought the world over.
Never eat at home, anyway. Not facing the sea.

Although sometimes the light will spill
into the window, and the horizon will frame
her ceramic face. Perhaps that's worse.

I should call my mother. Sort it out. Silly confusion.
Return it all. The reflected ocean framing Guanyin.

Echolocation

the last time I visited home,
I called your shape into the night five (5) times:

Once for poor luck,
like realising you hadn't studied
& had to cheat the exam; learning-
curve, running hard uphill, health
(1) check-up.

Twice for volume,
like an insect eaten by a metaphor
until the home hits home, nostalgia
in strange arms, winner of a wealth
(2) of tears.

the Next, like stasis,
vision obscured till all I saw were those
disappointed ejaculators, my ancestors;
crowding, clouding, haranguing me to a long life,
(3) sightless.

Fourth, I fell,
over drinks & art-chat, taken back
to second family's bed & set down
in sister Sharda's sheets; love & love of virtue,
(4) leaving.

& Last, nothing at all, entered
the way homonyms surrender into sound;
when the echo is the body, barely aware
of what spills. Such a peaceful death,
(5) my home.

Terminal

When you left me at the airport,
you named me as a liar. & my lies
are your armour, I know. The very best
are promises to God: tomorrow,
I'll be grateful. Tomorrow, I'll be
good. & tomorrow, so true.

At three a.m. before I woke you,
I packed my bags & wondered
why I keep finding salt-shakers
in every room. I thought, perhaps
I'm frightened of being possessed.
Keep the demons out. Is evil
guiltless or are we endless guilt?
But in practice, they're the same.

I sleep horribly here.
There's a possum in the ceiling,
apparently. So it's not the ghosts
that got me in the end. Except you –
how I thought to cry when you called me
your Jiangshi. I wanted to name you
Possum, but I've always been sickened
by cute nicknames, & it's close enough
to fiction for you to reject it.

One day I'm going to bury you
in a mound made out of quilts;
shake you there in trembling circles.
I will waste my salt in you.
Keep you in this ceiling; never
wrong you again. Afterwards:
try not to lie.

dogbite

you know I keep on

circling artificial lakes
like hurricane Dorothy;
and all the little dogs are

snapping at my ankles.
benevolent injectables
diminishing the bite;

I'll wait until I'm rabid.

wrest my shaking legs
into a cataclysmic event.
stop leaving food out for

triceratops-masked lovers;
see, each one's a puppy in
the right nostalgic light.

not saying I miss you too.

and any mask could tell you
extinction equals beauty.
and any dog could tell you

loneliness is violence;
and an infection's just
an invitation, sorry

to be such a pain.

Youth

A man, whose name I don't remember as soon as he has said it. My short-term memory forever hurtling backwards. Sometimes they will say, *you know we've met before, right?* Yes, but remind me. Remind me in great detail. Every time is a first time, if you believe hard enough. This man, for the first time. The way he settles in; fills the chair like an amdram Henry IV sinking past the throne. *Heavy is the head*, I want to say. Heavy is the head. His nudity lined with ancient, purpled scars. *Sexy*, I say. There had been an accident on the road. As a teenager. A teacher who had loved him as he shouldn't. Who he had loved in return, with the great obsession of the young. Falling to the earth had been the end of things; there was no way to explain why they were there, bodies torn up on the asphalt together. Nearly four decades wrapped around the torso of a man. Heavy is the heart. History falls out surgeon-voiced, told with no seduction. Our tongues: the cleanest of precision. The past is not here to change our minds. The past is simply here. This man, who guides me to the floor. The way my knees find the hardwood of ibis hotels the world over. *Don't touch*, he says. *Don't use your hands. Only your mouth*. This is how I'll *be his boy*. I want to laugh; youth wrapped around me. *I'm nearly thirty*, I remind him; forever hurtling backwards. *Pretend*, he says. *For me. Pretend you are the newest that you've ever been.*

my parents never let me watch *Event Horizon* as a child

because of the scene with their skins inside-out. This is reasonable parenting. The problem with having a well-observed inner life is you don't see anything worth knowing. Don't you walk away from me. I often hear writers describe autobiographical work as *their baby*. This is unreasonable parenting. Autobiography invariably takes place in that other dimension. Press play the mirror universe, where the scars are at last where you'd most expect them to be. Sucked out the airlock; here's dark in me. Anecdote as evidence. One day soon I will have packaged & sold every painful thing ever housed in my body. The night-hope of art: to finally run out of itself & be emptied into something else, like superannuation. Make your parents proud. Be liquid in everything; let your pupils bleed. When I think of myself, the script provides a grim sense of afterboding, which by definition cannot ever come before. On the way, we won't need these eyes to see. I find myself at an exhibition at a visual artist's home, on a mission to drink the free wine dry & leave empty-handed. Wrought-iron loops; a plinth which proudly states, *event horizon*. I say, of course – I know this movie. The artist slips into the nothing-space beside me. *No, no*, he says. *Event horizon. The point from which no light returns*. Curves of metal, like a baby. *You know*, the sculptor says, a subconscious tap of his fingers on the price; *sometimes I think the real event horizon … is inside us*. The void face-palms. Creation is finished. Sam Neill with no eyes.

human sacrifice made sexy

Sometimes I think, if I were an Aztec
I'd be just handsome enough to have
my heart cut out.

And if the British Middle Ages,
I'd be androgynous enough to
burn as a witch.

Today, if someone super-attractive
asked me to peel my own face off,
I'd absolutely do it.

I commit a murder every time I make eye contact.

If I had been Helen, all the ships would
have sunk. Alexander: the pretty good.
Alexander: just fine.

Marie Antoinette – better minus head.
Keep the guillotine going and save me
for foot fetishists.

Sometimes I suspect that not even
the 'bots that follow me on Instagram
think I'm good-looking.

I scroll through goop for Gwyneth's tips on how to die.

Sick Pretty

for Maddie Godfrey

romantics saying sickness, for the beautiful
sickness makes you beautiful

            the individual illness, articulated
tell me why we ought to feel protagonistic

when post-surgical stitching fails, and the first thing
I am hired to do upon remembering how to stand,
papery and bloodless, is pose heroic for a fashion spread

I want to be the obstacle
I want to be the mountain

when a man holds my disclosure tight in his bed
gazing with a thousand-faced romance, says: *there was someone*
I could have loved, but I was too afraid he'd make me sick.
I won't make that mistake again. I'll take care of you instead.

in any pair of eyes, the eyes of everyone rejected out of fear before

but tell me I'm too porcelain to abandon
as you finally fuck the ghost that got away

please tell me how I am an individual
when I can be reparation

                    first step: falling

I'm laid flat on my bed, again
   at least I can be pale, again
everything that holds still holds beneath me
slides behind my shoulder-blades
the small of my back

armoured with fragility
at our sickest, how we are desired

second: you are falling

fall past checkpoints, past migration laws,
past birthdays, AIDS Days, anniversaries,
past invisible, past thinning and wanted,
past the promise of a self –

am I struggling now to write because I'm sick
or because I no longer feel so sick and pretty?

this is not a metaphor –

cheekbones of doomed youth
should I not have read Genet at seventeen?
should I throw away my white-blonde copy of *Holding the Man*?
exorcisms for collarbones, for sentimentality
waking every morning a more verdant Linda Blair

sunshine: freckle me a little further
medicative, metronomic

finally, this is falling
backwards off a bridge between yourself and
yourself; landing one foot on the same bridge
and then falling.

Instructional

Proposition: ghosts are constantly eating you alive.

Quantifier: you do not have enough substance as a human being
to provide a ghost with any real nourishment.

1. you feel a ghost biting your lower lip.
2. you bite your lower lip.
3. your mouth is now a ghost.

4. you affix your bone structure somewhere along
the tipping-point between sexy and spooky.
5. you hear some ghosts mutter that they don't
find you sexy or particularly spooky.
6. you (non-verbally) invite the ghosts
to chew upon your eyeballs.

7. you take a selfie.
exposure: spooky. shadows: spooky/sexy.
cool-tone filters: you decide.
8. there is now both more and less of you to be consumed;
the universal quantifier, proved true and false, implodes.
there is no such thing as ghosts. now, you are the ghost.
9. you perform a throaty *ooo* and
jangle your imaginary chains
all the way into September.

here is what we have between us

for Koh Wan Ching

(The Esplanade, Singapore)

i.

(1) a reclaimed land /
we walk on water.

(2) the definition of embassy /
and stand here by design.

(3) a character: the critic
who lost her sanctuary.

(4) at nightclubs, there are rules
for drinking, rules for dice.

(5) another character we might
meet: the man still on his way.

(6) always, there is a dream of a home.

(7) PR notes on how and why
to annex body as terrain.

ii.

Laws also apply to foreigners living and working in Singapore. Being HIV-positive will classify a foreigner as a prohibited immigrant. The ban on HIV-positive foreigners entering on short-term visit passes was lifted on 1 April 2016. Tourists or short-term visitors are not required to undergo an HIV test. HIV testing is usually required for applying for a work pass, long-term visit pass, employment pass, or permanent residence. Those who are found to be HIV-positive will not be granted passes.

(Action for AIDS Singapore)

iii.

hello love.   so – a descending journey
instead of an escape.
what's lacking now
is really looking at
into the bile duct
as a way to cross

to hell. am I crazy? or are you keen on another try?

time is now. this
could have been
and this was that.
can you imagine?
we never know –
except to feel the water drain.

Leak

In Chinese folklore, Jiangshi is a hopping corpse; a rigid body feeding from the life force of the living. Vampiric, trampolining: you might know Jiangshi from Hong Kong cinema, or when a partner, in a spurt of colder anguish, names you as an abject mass of myth.

[30/01/2019] / *Confidential information of 14,200 people with HIV, including names, contact details and medical information, has been stolen and leaked online /*

It came to light / the culprit: HIV-positive, had not only used his boyfriend's blood to pass blood tests so he could work in Singapore, but / got hold / from the HIV registry which his doctor boyfriend had access to / failing

Although they have become a signifier of horror, the image of Jiangshi is thought to have originated from the bodies of migrant workers. During the Qing dynasty, those who died far from home would be tied upright to bamboo poles and transported through the night. As the bamboo flexed up and down, the dead appeared to hop together as they made their journey home.

to take reasonable care / The records leaked include those of 5,400 Singaporeans diagnosed with HIV up to January 2013, and 8,800 foreigners /

[The Straits Times]

Perhaps selfishly, when I read the news
my first thought was to check the dates.

Maria Tumarkin: *Time makes room for timelessness / Everything has already happened / The past does not move through the present like a pointed finger / The past is not 'told you so' / It is a knock on the door in the middle of the night. You open the door and no one is there*

My lover brings home a *bagua* mirror, though
we never find the time to nail it above the door.

In the unseen spaces between stories, you might carve yourself a shadow.

He tells me, you can't mourn for something
you could never hope to grip to. Bury home.
There is a kind of memory for naming other
truths as your own.

Where are we to place our individual traumas
in a legacy of expulsion? How might we best
refuse to move on home?

/ Kristeva tells us of a border tightening past the skin /

Perhaps foolishly, sometimes I wish to be
among them.   A history is hopping near.

When I was diagnosed, I understood the doctor had an obligation to report
it. Why was it that I stayed at least another six months without deportation?
Did she take pity on me, or did she forget? Was I not considered to be any
kind of threat? A blank space on a government list.

I can't let things go, and this may be
a blessing and a curse. A talisman to
the forehead, a stamp, another test.

Time seems very far away now, doesn't it?

Yuan Mei: *the sound of crackling flames / blood rushes forth / bones cry*

An axe. A broom. Black ink. Hold your
breath. Do you hear the bell? Abuse of
power, abuse of weakness.

Now the border // is the subject.

When I / you leave you / me,
a reminder of the mirror above   the entrance.
Do you hear it? I am longing
to be with you.   Hop.   Hop.
The country I have left is scratching at the door.

To have been there.
To have been missed.
But to have been there.

imagined nation

(East Perth, 2017)

If I were quizzed about my values,
I'd answer in the moments that
I value most: the endless meals
at Formosa, dated Taiwanese
singing contests idling in the back
part of my brain, or the time H
said 'I am Australian man',
wound down the window, shouting
'fuuuucking cuuunt!' as proof –

or when H said, 'maybe we
could get married one day.'
Or – I'm sorry – is this not
what this question means?
Perhaps these things are
un-translatable –

And quizzed upon my language
(which, decades on, I would not say
has been murdered – just FYI),
I might speak on the time H said
'I love you', and I, cheesy grin
and all, gave a shaky wǒ ài nǐ.

Or I might share the vocab
on H's desk I puzzled over:
bǎi wàn shēn jià *worth millions*
gé mìng xìng *revolutionary*
qǐng wù luàn rēng lā jī *please don't litter*
What they were for and why they
mattered mattering less than
that H wanted to learn them.

And if quizzed how best
to integrate: I so wished
it could be the eyes, held hands,
the tears, the maccas runs,
the break-ups, 5-year-plans,
the not-quite-sure, the
'what are we?', the whats-
app, fb messenger, line
'i miss u kiss u' come back –
draw a map between our bodies
and they might name it a failed
land but if there's a state of me
at all then name it yours.

Muad'Dib my veins, I'll go

after Migration: Like Paul Atreides *by Kenji C. Liu*

i.

This is a widening path –
to understand how heat makes
fresh messiahs in your blood.
Eventually, each limit longs to fall.
Pause-gospel, Paul; find necessary fictions

to spark along the same burnt road.
Mind-killer think the slow zoom in.
It's not enough to duct-tape rats to cats
& call it science fiction.
There has to be a price as well.

So dive me, little mouse.
Make double agents of the white.
Pandora any box squared deep within, & pain.
Sisters & political systems. Boy born
with all the hopes of witches.

All the rest shall flow from here.

Messiah, Muad'Dib; & other made-up words
like *immune system*; like *residence*,
or *nation state*. Spill them all
upon the sand. Now drink it in:
this drying, blue-eyed taste of kin. & entryways,

the worms. Feel the reverb; changing veins.
White blood cells going through a synthwave phase.
Pounding, Paul Atreides. Bare citizen
fucked with desert; killing-worded, named.

My passport reads, *your smallest moon.*
See: I breathe.
Irrhythmed here: the pulse of yet
another planet better left unknown.
Muad'Dib me, & I'll go.

Otherwise, how sand will swallow.

ii.

In utero, like nirvana, the ancestry ingesting. All memory of all forebears flooding in. How the lens begins to glow. Again, a birth. Soft power: stacked into the eyes. Identified so easily in blue. Remember how it feels, knowing just enough. A needle to the neck of comfort. Replication, genealogy: these things take precision. Growth: another careless thing. Hissing, here, the kind of monstrous made with no becoming. Were-worm howling past a hidden moon. Remember all the lives that mound beneath the skin. Sex-kitten, tyrant, ghoul; make me sister to myself. Now she presses down dissent. Possessed of lazy tropes; at least you know. Trial of abomi*national performance of tears*. Finish young & beautiful. Eat the young & eat the beautiful. Let someone else walk blindly into history – we have to keep suppression on our many minds within. Poor Alia, there's room left in me yet to chase a wet reality. Each time recalled anew it means returning home. Time: the last residence offered us. Remember how

the network fails to break. Now she flings herself from the parapet. Fly, bad baron; fly on by. The sand's still white, the sand's bright blue.

(paradise)

Ancestor Poem

sometimes it occurs to me
that somewhere between seroconversion & diagnosis
I inherited perhaps dozens of bloodlines, dozens of lives

the perfect viral memory tunnelling forward through time
        rude '81 to present day

& maybe each one of them was as frightened & alone as I was

            & as unforgiving of themselves

            & some of them are still alive

            & some or more are probably gone

& I'll never have a single memory of any of them
                        not even when I pretend.

& maybe it occurs to me
I should be able to look down at veins beneath my skin
                            I take a moment

just to feel the way they're flowing

& while I'm there, remember
            something of someone whose blood
            now lives to multiply in me

                    & I know how this sounds:

like every third episode of *Star Trek*

like some kind of B-grade comedy
in which I'm haunted by a group of sassy homosexual ghosts
            they give me dating advice & help me get the man

but I just want something small:

a scent from their childhood
a crush that didn't break their heart
a halfway-decent birthday
I want to remember 1991

Elizabeth Freeman writes about a Queerness
persisting over time
& when I think of HIV-time, both the HIV & time tend toward collapse –
like Tim Dean writing of transmission
as a promise to explode a single notion
of a future

time sits next to itself

& the archive is dividing

in packages of 30 pills
each one a waiting body long before
they become body

& I don't think I care for tragedy

except for what here now
persists in me

a promise to explode

to never cry at a lazy poem again
choreograph all the things I can't remember
& all my B-grade *Star Trek* futures

& it's just like when my mother warned me
she didn't think I had the resilience for living with HIV

but it's like, you know what, mum, who even has the time
for resilience anymore

all I need is a calendar with today's date on it
& we're good.

Anna Paquin

(April 2020)

I think about how in the movies, the first boy who kissed you fell into a coma, and you learnt the hard way that proximity = death. His veins bulged out like ingénue eyes, and the movie kept on going. You were so young, Anna; you didn't know what nearness meant. How you got into a car with Hugh Jackman and your life changed forever: you became the least useful member of a super-powered squad, give or take the guy with laser eyes. If I had laser eyes, Anna, I'd probably destroy my apartment; I'd crumble with the walls. Maybe I'd cope better with the distance if I also got a jet and a fancy name. The other day, I was forced to take the train to a pointless job interview, and a man spat near me. I wanted to scream until I burst wide open, but I reminded myself that he was just an extra, and I get to be Rogue. Still, the horror of it hits in waves. // Anna, I never really appreciated before now that wearing gloves could become a cornerstone of your personality, but lately I've been thinking that anyone can reach out and touch nothing. You're not the only one who can define yourself by a crisis hairstyle. I could be gently iconic, if only on the 'gram. Yes, Anna Paquin, I plan to be both brazen and timid with my loneliness, just wait and see. But if I'm being honest, Anna, I didn't think my cool mutant future would turn out like this. Every time I took a BuzzFeed quiz, they told me I was Storm. // Anna, I think about the way your Southern Gothic telepathic powers made you fear the noise of other minds, until the plot instructed you to fall for the first vampire that walked your way. Academy Award-winner Anna Paquin, why are so many of my poems about vampires? Vampires and mutation. Is it because I'm desperate for the change, or terrified of it? I keep a prop coffin in my living room, and a prop candle by my bed. Nothing feels real anymore, except, of course, until it is. Recently, a tweet told me that all the social isolation was negatively affecting the psychic vampire community, and I couldn't stop thinking about it. How do you even stake a psychic vampire? Then I went to the bathroom and caught my reflection in the mirror and thought, *oh*.

afterwards, bring me back as Winona Ryder's accent in *Dracula*

I have a crush. Look at me: I'm not like other boys. I make jokes from '92 while getting fucked. Cuddle up in Eiko Ishioka. Throw myself at tragic backstories, text *uwu* mid-ironically. Wide-eyed hellmouth; naïve vortex; *Jigoku*-inspired bottom. There's a searching wobble in my tone. Script desperate cinema in letter form. You'll say, *don't fall in love with me*. Gag on you. I'll vanish when you do. & here's another joke!! Two Poz friends start a book club, & every month it's *Dracula*, again. One turns to the other & says, *when it starts we all think we're Lucy, but we always end up Mina.* (Mina has no punchline) So please: I'm seeking out a rounded vowel. Desiring upwards with a lizard crawl. & quietly, quietly: I used to be so fearful of sex. I think the many whispering parts of me still are. & more softly, still: would things be any different if my life weren't woven tight around it? In absence & in gain? Maybe if I hadn't spent so much of my twenties trying to describe myself as a twink, I might better know how a letter goes on living? But there's no Grindr tribe for *starlet, falling*. Unfulfilled desire is the autopsy of innocence; like holding a wake in your heart for bookmarked porn stars as they age out. It's the urst between things that aren't there: fan fiction & youth. & last letter: when I was a teen, I scoured the web for pictures of Keanu Reeves' dick. I never found any, but jerked off to the expectation, anyway. Thank you, to an image that did not exist, & never needed to.

Gorgon

for Finn O'Branagáin

i.

yesterday my shoulders seized up
exhaustion seeping past my eyes
I want to cry my body out of itself
into liquid. somehow preserve my
bone-dry hair, my gums.

this morning I thought I might tie my hair
in tiny knots, as if I were some lesser Björk,
but maybe all I'd be is scalp.

sing no words but keep a sound
find flow in sad-man demonstration
steady-cam the soft-snake gaze
make a path to the procession
act more to notice less.

ii.

off-weight always falling
walk skewing like a crab
zero core & all extremity
shake. then hug. locate
a mermaid-spine – rose
and banana to the base
before the drums begin –

iii.

this morning, when I lifted the blinds,
it felt like I was seeing the sun for the
first time in months. for a second, and
still maybe now, I felt I could be finally
ready to melt.

iv.

itching scratched into my hands,
my feet; the pus of some pimple
or some bite marking my kneecap
like a milk-white eye. at breakfast
I obsess over a matted knot in my
hair, while a man over the speakers
raps pussy, pussy, pussy. *can't*
believe it's only been two days,
says Michelle. sometimes you see
them glance away, avert their eyes,
turn to their partners like *what have*
you brought me to? but sometimes
one will plant their eyes to face you,
like: I know what this is. I see; go on.
go on, go on, gorgon, before I'm gone.

v.

at the aquarium today:
    all those jellyfish
    pufferfish, lionfish, stonefish
    degrees of pain for poison

an octopus stuck to the glass
a coiled sea-snake, hidden face
a starfish in a child's hands

    nurse sharks
    the stingrays
    a sea turtle larger than any of them

and later at home:
    Uma Thurman
    Jolin Tsai
    a shot of Harry Hamlin

staring at reflected clay.

you came home with purple hair

and your platinum length had disappeared
I saw the darkening mauve you'd made
your colour in my sternum, cracking
because I know for some Queers, a haircut is the best we have
to heal that thing grown tired inside of us.

you came home, cropped purple hair
and clearly this meant moving on
as much as it meant cutting off
before you arrived, I spent a choking hour packing what was yours
folded up your shirts, held tight that

stupid husky hat I always made you wear
the photo of your vanished mother
kept hidden with your socks
wondering if perhaps she hacked her hair away after she'd left you
and how, before too long, I'll be your spectre, too.

you came home to tell me I was not your home
the thought of me had broken in you
and somehow, you had come to hate
and I can't help thinking it's clichés that cut the deepest
when all I could say was how I loved your hair –

and you said, *thank you.*

I used to wake each morning and look for you
by signifiers on the bedside table
your cologne, your portable charger
that bottle of bleach you kept there, ever ready to be used
but I was more afraid of losing than of loss.

now, of course, the bedside table's bare
I train my eyes to hold
sight of your fading shade
I'm learning how to live Han purple, trailing to Egyptian blue
and still I keep it growing

notes on *The Exorcist*

in my dreams I call von Sydow daddy
stick out stone tongues and learn a little Swedish

so desperate to impress. but the man's a carving
like my mother, Max von Sydow: even his palest

doubts are staunch – John Wayne of holy water
we play chess in other movies, all the while

that awful girl spouts obscenities in bed
and Burstyn's looking tired – so tired

I long for us to snap together, all these years apart
vomit in the cinema, owl-headed, overwrought

instead I press rewind; imagine spooning God
I wish I cared for Catholics the way I care for

baby devils, but I don't.

public health the silence of god

TELEHEALTH

registrar calls to say, *I know the phone seems strange. How are you?* Since for years, the best way you could bear a clinic wait was cast it as a Bergman film, & now: to sit at home. Reply, *not quite sure where I am*, except it looks like here: the drain-aged epidemic as a new pandemic starts to rain.

WHISPERING

phlebotomist, misplace your bloods. Collect, repeat. Bibi Andersson; no persona. Need to know you're still the same. Three weeks, three phone calls: no reply. *Outpatient* is an awful word. But you know doctors: silence means there is no change. So practise every scene inside. Your Swedish: prophylacted. God's so quiet this century   sonata in HIV.

INGMAR,

how the months roll by, & now: to take the bus. Body on a public route. A different registrar will buzz your pocket, speaking *early.* You tell him that you're coming in. *Any specific issue you have to see me in person for?* Specific issue is you want to be there in person. This crawling irritation: God, have you become your grandmother? Except Alison could never have accepted her strange baby should live longer than his strange infection –

[close-up]:

for the five years or so before she passed, Alison would proclaim with a terrible certainty that this Christmas would be her last. it was almost funny: how many times to be wrong, just to be proven right. & then, there was the last: lost in her body. unable to move, unable to speak. a different illness & a different time. silence, still …

CLIMBING

stairwells, like you always do. The Pavlov-comfort in returning to a place you thought you should despise. Another registrar jokes, *how's that for service?* First time on human record immunology is running before the clock. He opens files; he taps on keys. He says, *here's something odd. Looks like we have no blood from you since eighteen months ago.* Except – how can that be? When you so easily recall those days you've sat before appointments; all the ways you've been assured. What happened to evidence? All those results; scripted to their mouths between. Revolving-doctor: unconcerned. Lack of communication. *Sometimes tests will fall into* the vault; *they never reach the file we see.* He tells you, *why not go again today?* & then: you'll know. Pull the stairs down as you leave.

HANDSOME

phlebotomist, collect with ease. Chat up trainees as the colour pools. Say, used to it now; but I'll never get it exactly right, you know? You ask how long it takes to learn. How many years before you could empty yourself instead? How long just to find a vein? Think of it as a party trick. Think of it as editing. Now cut the future, phone will ring: some new voice tells you, quiet same. Receive it. Receive it like piano keys. Close-up of the verb for faith. The body-work shudders to its next long take, & still: you faith –

But sometimes, I am left to wonder … where is this vault?
Is it beneath the hospital? Undergrounded; hiding from the light?
What locks keep it closed?
Who walks it; stacks it; sweeps its floors?
What future longs to launch it from the earth?
Am I there now? … bodied in reams of paper?

Call out into the bright. Of course, the point is no reply.
No science, & no fiction.
I wish Bergman had made *Star Trek* instead.
If I ever die, shoot Liv Ullmann into space.

Nothing

I think about you, Zero. Your punk tattoos; your skin; your spit; your bright and beaming eyes. The deep, infective joy each time you recognise a Pokémon. The girlfriend who keeps you, happy to be your partner visa – if nothing else. So far away, in pre-pandemic time: the final night with you inside. You said it felt like you would break me. I always thought that's what poets wanted. Something shattered. Something, to be nothing.   Months later, somewhere in the city, I passed you in the light. You looked so disappointed in me. Or maybe, Zero, only tired. Gave my ass a half-hearted squeeze and faded into the evening. All moments are irreducible, but so many have a warrant out on forgetting. Time keeps calling the cops on memory. This moment is already Zero.   And later still: like droplets seeking distant rooms, a text from you; a touch of nowhere. *I'm scared of getting sick. So scared of going home. Scared nobody will want me inside of them again.* Zero, no one ought to break in two. Now, most nights, I just want to go to sleep. The longing yawn of skin to skin. What power within the fake name that you gave me: Zero, Zero, Zero.   Just now, I walked a moment in the air to think: is this a different night from any I remember? Returning to my bed, a moth appeared from deep within the folding void of my pocket. The moth flew broad grey circles, narrowing toward the light – like it hadn't even read about Icarus as a child. But then, I've also known myself to mistake a shuddering bulb for sun. How willingly we hold ourselves hostage to the lonely volts of others. Slight disturbances of light; the speed of our vibration. The need – then disappearance. Zero, there's no craft in this work; except the way exhaustion's always there, splitting the proud corners of poems.

in season 2 episode 17 of *Buffy the Vampire Slayer*, Ms Calendar tries to restore Angel's soul

always   there's a curse   either
one is cursed   or   one
is the curse   time leaves no middle
ground as dire   as random acts   or
agency   *hey, come outside*   invite
me in   the curse involves a soul   its loss
like any work   a soul   & loss
      Angel's lost his vampire soul
            he doesn't want it back

cold open   here   I call you in
no one dances with their friends   no one
narrates   no running through the woods   good
deeds   just my disclosure   you agree
      you know what undetectable means
& I agree   I'm sure you say   you've taken
PrEP   you fuck so hard   I think in dreams
but afterwards   hour of the wolf   drive to
emergency   for PEP   you in
the waiting room   me wrapped in bed
      you tell me that I ought to pay

& I do   because I was the one
      with the illness   & I knew
that we were going to love each other

   & if I'm thinking about first times
   it's sort of like   arm-wrestling destiny
   & just like any   one-night-stand
   & mostly   plotline begging to begin
      hey, come outside   invite me
in   the ritual there won't be the breath to speak

sketch impressions   haunt &
shift our   sleepless bodies   posed on
paper   go too fast   we try
new things   like lies   like debt   like

ownership like little dogs psychotic
breaks a matching haircut swift demise
& I do not mean to obscure the worst of me
but memory is another macguffin sometimes
it glows sometimes it shatters before it can
be used & either way the curse

& walking in & out of lives
it's sort of like how the actor playing Angel
got the role because he was literally so hot
a casting agent pulled him off the street & made
mysterious-vampire-brooding-boyfriend gold
which in turn is not dissimilar to Grindr
except on Grindr you don't earn residuals
when you hit syndication
often all you're left is residue

a silent year & you return so
thin so hard a quiet blame
I say I'll be there for you now make up for
all the terrible things I must have done
not just to you each lonely thing
think technopagan trouble-shoot our
secrets stakes & doomed amends
the art of imaginary translation
dark classroom writing's on the
wall & when you pass out in fire
over my floor watch you all night
& when you wake your fury such
cold disappointment that I didn't have the balls
to go there with you

but don't you see? I'm halfway fridged already

Angel's giving chase
he's working up an appetite
the past is not a choose-your-own-adventure
even though it is a little different every time
even if sometimes we can see what's coming

here you've come to say goodbye
it's over so you're leaving town *hey, come*
outside invite me in you hover
at the gate the door for
one last battle one last chance to tell me
all the ways that I was wrong & still to shout *the past is*
dead when I reply push uninvited
through the house before I find the
sound or fight in me to stop you –

you flush my antiretrovirals down the drain.

you knew by heart where I kept my pills
to remember it now, the staging seems almost rehearsed

& then you leave

see? the past's undead.

& sometimes I think, couldn't we do the one instead
where Xander becomes a hyena or whatever
some filler episode like that
I hate the way we choose to serve the plot
how many vampires I have written into being

I wish I could let go of things more easily
even though we both know that can't be entirely true
still isn't it enough to grieve your horror?
still I know there are no vampires & no one is cursed
still I could have seen it coming from a mile away
& still each time this episode plays

I can't help myself but think
Angel shows his fangs he growls he chases down his prey
& then he doesn't even bite her??
it's like shouldn't he be hungry?
why would he not want to drink her blood??
he just lets her snap & fall.

Drain

(after he flushes my antiretroviral medication)

for the toilet, which remains.

You: the afterlife of meds. This ever-present porcelain event. A body made, and then un-made. How many centuries of public works – new intimacies for moving water – before the moment my one-month reserves are tipped into that river-mouth? You are anti-poetry; but you hold it when you must. The proof is in your soaking absence. Imagine little whirlpools. How swiftly next days are re-sequenced into pipe. How the body must be partly made of drain. You are anti-memory; running ocean in a shallow bowl. Does anything still live in you, except dead weapons meant to come alive in me? To see a waterfalling future; and to resist. To quietly replace myself. Goldfish, once more made to swim. I surround you with preparations. I so long to be an act of service. You are anti-atmosphere; you: the transformation. You: slow maintenance of the same –

and lately I have had this feeling that the longer living goes, the harder it has been to remember if I've taken that day's meds or not. Mornings sliding out from me. For the first few years each pill must have felt so decisive, but for some time now – since the flush, at least – I seem to be swallowing up the day before I can process any sense of certainty that I have done so. I've taken to writing myself a note the moment my medication hits my mouth, and now my apartment is covered in post-its. Monday, yes and Tuesday, yes and Wednesday, on it goes … but that's time for you, isn't it? Time ceaselessly confirms itself. And when it overfills: to drain.

as if you were a pharaoh

i.

Leaving the cinema, J and I walk by wetlands, hands held against the trace of Hollywood's tears. *Don't you think*, I ask of the film, *that he was really a bad man?* An ibis wanders by the edges of my vision. *No, baby*, J responds. *I think he was a very sick man.* I agree, then let it go. The ibis hits the centre of my sight. I tell J we call the bird *bin chicken*. He repeats the phrase slowly and then nods, satisfied that this is true. *In my country*, he says, *there are no more*. Half-mournful and half-laugh: *because we ate them all*. I'm not sure how he means for me to react, but I cry at a lot of jokes – and I guess I cry at tragedies, too.

ii.

south of this place,

what love you bear
is stomped with grapes.
old soil enforced, returning
with a newfound ease.

and truth: it leans too close.

keep house content, then
shut your sheep-mind down.
all that pressure – lightning
storms that never strike.

you make a river, which
shall never reach the sea.

violence is elastic.

numbered here, the dirt-white flock:
grown thirteen, twelve, and ten, and eight.

iii.

The far-stretched beak: curved into a mud-black scythe. Match the balding head; the shade that sprints along the neck to cede the black for feather-white. And then, the deep-skinned red, ringed in orbits, rounding eyes; or tucked away beneath the wings. A long-clawed foot, sharp-scaled and resting gently on a set of scales. The bones of fish are made to slide inside, bathed in garbage; waterfalls of disappearance. More pressure on the rust-gold scales, and a croak escapes to hover with the urban breeze. Perhaps it sounds like: *Everyone is sick. Not everyone mistakes a shotgun for a sneeze.* And now the bird tips forward to the liquid waste; delicately tastes the murk. And there:

nesting somewhere beyond death, the wet-
lands slowly drain; anticipate the quake.

Aesthetics (new Sodom)

I want something ugly. Today I put another work online, and my friend messaged me to say: *I'm sorry for the violence. How beautiful you've turned it into art.* But what has beauty ever done for us, except maintain the same? Enough time passes, and we give the ugliness away. And I'm sorry, Pasolini, but I've come to realise I don't give a fuck about *Salò*. So great a flaw, to moralise over any frame that dares to move, and yet – I'd like to be as compositionally evil as the movie *Mamma Mia*. We look away. I want something half-dissected shut-your-eyes the many-bodied ugly. Transmission without metaphor. Seroconversion, with nothing nice to say. I want something that poetry can't have. I want to say: *not this time, poetry*. Not this time. I want to hold it tight, like the as-yet-undiagnosed rash spreading 'cross my torso. Mottled red: a smudging parody of snakeskin. No, it sounds too beautiful, still. Like: ibis-necked. Like: public health. Hold tight my ulcered inner cheek: remind me all the viral space I've yet to swallow up. Grunting *this is not a wound for use*. Like: first time I saw you scratch that redding dot, the elbowed angle of your arm. The horror when I realised. The awful shame when you saw what I was seeing. The way I asked what you'd let pierce your skin: like not asking at all. The flat-toned things we know to be true. The anguish on your face. The aesthetic perfection of the spiral. Erase my judging eyes and write: my love. *It's not your fault our cities are collapsing, but we don't have the luxury of becoming salt.* Instead: the glazing lens. Don't turn back now. See: the way I'm failing here, again. Don't look. Your stricken silence: how it made cruel cinema of you. Too beautiful. Too, too beautiful. You looked like a man of glass. How someone, in some past, would have painted angels. Like how one should imagine swans.

Judith & her unnamed attendant behead Holofernes in his bed

This one's just a story. He fucked me & I needed him. Surely that's enough. Desire, for me, comes wrapped up with delay. The two of them: they're kin. Perhaps I had to feel that love was to be won. He was a dealer & a $worker, which is only to say he knew what it is to sell perfection, however temporary. In the passenger seat in pitch-dark driveways, what closeness I wanted was always with the source of light. In any house: another unimportant mystery. He lived visa to visa, & I loved him because elsewhere, I have also been an unkind stay. He asked if I'd follow him to Taiwan. We'd get married; start a coin laundry. I'd work the day & he'd keep night. See, the dreams: they make a double-edge of little lives. So few places left to live, except a here & now.

> The last time we were together, I broke an unexceptional silence. Disclosure is to bare a throat, though not always your own. I told him I couldn't follow him because I was Poz. There are distances, & then there's distance. He said he'd guessed as much. He said, & so was he. I hadn't guessed at all. I said, *so we're the same.* Twelve long months we'd kept our quiet. He held me in his arms & said, *but it's different. My first boyfriend tricked me; lied to me, then left me. I got it because I loved someone. You probably got it because you couldn't be careful. See: I didn't deserve it.* All I say is, *I'm not sure.*

Slip away to fiery dawn. Waiting for the king to rise. There are paintings of this, I know. Body-blade-body stacked with care; beheaded to a waking light. Here, we were supposed to be kin. Assurances made; a Revelation. Shouldn't we be of a kind? But as I pulled him closer in, chest yearning toward chest, I'd never felt more alone. More locked within the limit of a single body. Two breathing documents of proof, & yet: time's shallow flutter. The deep inhale, & nothing.

to become brush-stroke / still beheading / name
the second hand gripped on the hilt / to bring
down empire / paint a speculative fiction of the
past / canvas-bodied / selling, sold.

Every time I long for something beneath touch,
I remember: there is one perfect sword moving
deep within us. Death to any sleeping king. Life now
to servants, waiting for their names.

Some days, I find his profile picture on Facebook. His spotless skin upright in white hotel sheets. He looks like money. Limit. Silence.

It is only a picture.   Nothing here is moving.

Eris

You sat in my lap, trying out a toothless bite on my index finger. With my other hand, I flicked through the pages of a book about shapeshifting.

As follows:

a plush toy python, a rubber pterodactyl, the tear ducts
of a drunk emotion; a much-cuddled octopus named
Colin and the squid I'd purchased in New Zealand as his
rival (though I can only recall the name given to Colin);

paint smeared on walls, pairs of oversized sunglasses
and possible tantrums at Dog Swamp shopping centre;
books on the occult borrowed and visits long-delayed,
changes recognised and tracked by way of Instagram,

the uncertain shape in the crib on the monitor, the peace
and the unrest of listening for the sound of sleeping;
the much-tormented plastic of a doll, jealousies and
generosities discovered in becoming an older sibling;

a Tree of Life painting left unfinished, an impression
of a family at a baby shower, and the gold-dipped ram
now sitting atop my dresser … everyone that will never
be known; the inevitability of damage, the expectation,

egos, hopes placed and misplaced, my deep limitations,
inflated sense of collective responsibility, an ideal only,
a burst of soap bubbles and somebody else's future
(which is constantly arriving, and yet may never arrive)

in which the shifting space from one shape to the next
is a multitude of microscopic acts of repair; from chaos.

Arrival Time [in fifteen movements]

i. I know myself to reach any destination ten to fifteen minutes faster than Google Maps will ever believe of me. My boyfriend calls it gay pace. I can't help it. I have places to be, and more places not to be. Everywhere, I'm early.

ii. The late José Muñoz begins *Cruising Utopia* by telling us, *Queerness is not yet here.*

iii. A quick search on Urban Dictionary describes gay pace as the incredibly fast rate at which gay couples progress their relationships. A slightly more drawn-out search suggests we walk gay pace for fear of judgement, or attack. A confidence coach said this. Perceived risk, is what she said.

iv. Ten years ago I'd throw my body between knife fights in Northbridge. Those three a.m. heroics: they slow us down. Somehow, I always talked them out of it a hundred or so seconds before police would dare arrive. Why, at my most precarious, did I feel indestructible? Still – is it too much to ask for an innocence that makes men drop their weapons?

v. I've either become wiser, or more fragile –
which I suppose aren't mutually exclusive
things, even if it feels like they ought to be.

vi. Now, as I remind myself how to drive, I'm working hard to beat that flight-flight panic of approaching cars and faces as they reach me in the rear-view mirror. I have to constantly remind myself that this is just how traffic works. Everything is just movement across networks, through space. The inner map I make of unrecognised faces.

vii. On the drive to Girrawheen Senior High, a woman on Classic FM tells me that it only takes sixty seconds for a blood cell to circuit the whole body, and all I can think is: *How dare. The nerve.*

viii. Cells are constantly moving, HIV is constantly multiplying, antiretrovirals are constantly suppressing, borders are constantly extending. Every environment can safely be described as *hostile.*

ix. At the school, I try to teach the students about tempo, and I realise that I've begun to think of them as *mine.* To me, they seem so indestructible.

x. Donna Haraway keeps reminding me to *stay with the trouble*, except I'm wondering if the movement is the trouble.

xi. (I very rarely read critical theory past the introduction.)

xii. Every time a man on Grindr walks into my home, it is with the awareness that I'm putting myself at risk of murder or of harm. The way we trade in false proximities. This is how they bind us: perhaps we truly put ourselves at risk of care.

xiii. Kinship: another *perceived risk.*

xiv. Someone told me recently that they had never really considered what borders meant, until they closed. I tell them that when I was diagnosed positive, I eventually came to realise there was nowhere I could go but home.

xv. At Galup, I force myself to slow to look at birds. *Arrival* has so many other meanings by the lake. Just three or so kilometres around. I am trying to find in circumnavigation some sense of Queer belonging, what Elizabeth Freeman describes as *persisting over time*. Inside me, everything I claim to know spreads a little further away. Where best to fall within that rippling diagram?   To be Queer is to understand you have been someplace you will never return. In a few months' time, I might wait to see the children hatch. The way ducklings learn to swim: zooming to their mothers in impossible bursts. Baby birds always feel as if they're mine, especially in the way they speed away.

Treatment [/ / 2021]

as an investment in my future happiness
I will buy a thousand bootleg Pikachus
read Kristeva in every waiting room; never on the way home
& talk to the leftover goths on the Fremantle line
markering their love affairs, fresh politics in poster print
who make unprompted jokes about STIs
& I will smile kindly, because – sure, sex can be funny, I agree
& who hasn't wanted to laugh with all that they enfold

today, after seven years of blood tests
I feel for the first time a sharp & wearying sting
on entry   & then it passes
take note of every yearning smallness
to be tiny is meaningful enough
it is a slow growing –
re-making intimacy day to day

I feel a little faint
the blood-drawn nurse asks three times
if I'm the type who needs to lie down
as if she forgets each time
I read an article about youths in China who must *lie down*
lie down against a crunching world
to protest when nothing you know is standing
I need to lie down

I so rarely considered how much time
it takes just to be permanently sick
the constant state of surprise
even without matter to detect

from now on when I speak of treatment
I will include desire not as a past event
but a fixture of the future. a persistent truth

when I am formless
when I am charged with sparks
settling with the sideways determination
of an orgy at the Scarborough hotel
there are things I miss about myself
from the balcony to the dawn
gasping once again at water
& re-imagining the fall

lie quietly across tomorrow
another sun is breathing here
beneath me, grass articulates
I will not absolve you of the risk
this is something everyone does for themselves
above me, un-shaped birds are verbing
young mothers practice boxing in the park
I store myself away, undescribed
planting   held   another hit.

I will be something other than resilient
a new & care-full virality
how peaceful to forget the word *recover*
no, I cannot absolve you of your risk
but I can pass by you. gentle. lick your sweat
& remember there is ocean kept between us
add me to your list. please. it will all be worth it.

The *Little Mermaid* [left unfinished]

Antony and the Johnsons, 'Hope There's Someone'.
Virginia Woolf, *The Waves*.
A stage direction reads: *bathed in gold light*.

A text about the Southern Ocean, pectorals, and hammerhead sharks.
A stage direction reads: *she puts the hook into her mouth*.
A character says, 'love is death.'

Beyoncé, 'Crazy in Love'.
A stage direction reads: *each one clamouring to be heard*.
A character says, 'at human heat already!'

Björk, 'Pluto'.
A placeholder for choreography; a placeholder for critical theory.
A text that is spoken in the voice of a princess.

A stage direction reads: *she places her hands on his chest*.
Judy Chicago, early feminist works.
A stage direction reads: *produces fish-food and puts some in the tank*.

A text about capitalism, the erotic, and having a weak voice.
A character says, 'love is pain.'
A mirror ball; a lip-synch; a slow dance; a curse.

A character says, 'you will feel the corpses of all of those loves grasping at you.'
Judy Garland, 'Smoke Gets in Your Eyes'.
A sequence that's been given up on; left unfinished.

A stage direction reads: *her face in a shallow puddle*.
A character says, 'I want to drown in the arms of my pain.'
An ocean that has frozen over; a message in a bottle; a Korean restaurant; a kiss.

A character says, 'and always left unfinished.'
José Esteban Muñoz, *Cruising Utopia*.
A stage direction reads: *bodiless in the sky*.

Anohni, 'Paradise'.

Paradise

for Joe Lui

I wonder if we don't sometimes
confuse exhaustion
for a kind of love

but I would drip fatigue
down our worn-out length
if it would be enough

to keep us bound; but reaching –

yearning for the next,
and grasping our disquiet
for anything that's left

like ibises, like longkangs
our newness drooling
into drains –

when spreadsheets might express concern

I pray that what we've
always done is hold
tight to a blinding life

un-build the kind of world
we'll never see, but know
like skin stretched out on floors

that place worth screaming down the mic

where we shatter love like sleep
or fuck like sheep; co-parenting
three-headed beasts

who'll grow to feast on paradise
love's tired-place – where words
fall down; and grapes applaud

and everybody knows us – except, thank god, for us.

Notes

Many of these poems are densely referential and if you are so inclined, I hope Google can be your friend. Similarly, I have not provided a glossary of terms related to the experience of living with HIV. For further information, I recommend engaging with organisations like NAPWHA, WAAC, Action for AIDS Singapore, or similar non-government organisations related to HIV/AIDS advocacy.

'137 near Trujillo': this poem refers to a mass child sacrifice in pre-Incan Peru, reported on in 2018.

'Treatment [3/12/14]', 'Treatment [20/12/14]', 'Treatment [26/05/15]': the text of these poems is extracted from correspondence I sent over the first months of antiretroviral treatment.

'we go camping in the woods with the most derivative witches': Pazuzu is the name of the devil that possesses the child Regan in the 1973 film *The Exorcist*, which stars Linda Blair, Ellen Burstyn and Max von Sydow.

'I watch the student actors perform *Angels in America* the day after I am diagnosed positive': Paddy Chew (1960–1999) was the first Singaporean person to come out publicly with HIV/AIDS. He was the subject and performer of The Necessary Stage's *Completely With/Out Character*, staged in 1999. Rochor is the area in Singapore which contains LASALLE College of the Arts. Xiqu is the term for traditional Chinese opera. I was offered a scholarship to study a Masters of xiqu and intercultural theatre at the Shanghai Theatre Academy, which was rescinded due to my HIV status.

'Sick Pretty' sites itself in response to Susan Sontag's seminal text *Illness as Metaphor*. It also makes reference to fantasy author and editor Vida Cruz's critique of Joseph Campbell's *The Hero with a Thousand Faces;* to the works of Jean Genet and *Holding the Man* (1995) by Timothy Conigrave, and to *The Exorcist* film.

'here is what we have between us': the quote in part ii is taken from the Action for AIDS Singapore website. AfA is a non-government organisation in Singapore formed in response to HIV/AIDS.

'Leak': a bagua mirror is a protective amulet hung above an entryway, used in classical feng shui to ward off negative energy. This work refers to Julia Kristeva's *Powers of Horror: An Essay on Abjection* (Columbia University Press, 1984). The quote from Yuan Mei is from the 1788 text *Zi Bu Yu / What the Master Would Not Discuss*. This particular translation was freely accessible on the internet.

'imagined nation': this poem was written in response to citizenship rules and the 'values test' for migrants implemented by the Turnbull government in 2017. It also makes reference to comments made by right-wing Senator Pauline Hanson.

'Muad'Dib my veins, I'll go': part i of this poem sites itself around the character of Paul Atreides, who is the protagonist of Frank Herbert's 1965 science-fiction novel *Dune*. Part ii refers to the character of Alia, Paul's sister, in the sequels *Dune Messiah* (1969) and *Children of Dune* (1976).

'Ancestor Poem': this poem refers to work from Queer academics Elizabeth Freeman and Tim Dean, who are otherwise referenced in the book's epigraph and in the poem 'Arrival Time'.

'Anna Paquin': this poem was written at the beginning of the Covid pandemic and refers to two properties in which Anna Paquin is a leading actor: the *X-Men* films and the HBO series *True Blood* (2008–2014). In *X-Men*, the character Rogue takes from the life force of anybody she touches.

'Winona Ryder': Eiko Ishioka is the costume designer for Francis Ford Coppola's *Bram Stoker's Dracula* (1992), starring Winona Ryder as Mina. *Jigoku* is the title of a 1960 Japanese horror film, which translates to 'hell'.

'Gorgon': this poem is drawn from a journal I kept as a performer during the season of *Medusa* by Finn O'Branagáin in 2018.

'Arrival Time' refers to three texts: José Esteban Muñoz, *Cruising Utopia: The Then and There of Queer Futurity* (New York University Press, 2009); Donna Jean Haraway, *Staying with the Trouble: Making Kin in the Chthulucene* (Duke University Press, 2016); and Elizabeth Freeman, *Time Binds: Queer Temporalities, Queer Histories* (Duke University Press, 2010).

Acknowledgements

Epigraphs on p. 5: © 2001 by Justin Chin, from the poem 'Undetectable', published in the book *Harmless Medicine* (Manic D Press: San Francisco). Used with permission of the publisher; © 2011 by Tim Dean, from the essay 'Bareback Time', published in the book *Queer Times, Queer Becomings*, editors E.L. McCallum and Mikkho Tuhkanen (State University of New York Press). Used with permission of the publisher. Excerpt on page p. 55, © 2018 by Maria Tumarkin, from *Axiomatic* (Brow Books). Used with permission of the author. Earlier versions of poems in this collection have been published in Australian Poetry's *Best of Australian Poems 2021, Baby Teeth Journal, Birdcoat Quarterly, Cordite Poetry Review, Crab Fat Magazine, EXHALE: An Anthology of Queer Voices from Singapore* (Math Paper Press), FDBN (Sticky Fingers Publishing), *From Whispers to Roars, Grieve* anthology, volume 7 (Hunter Writers Centre), *Lite Lit One, Mantissa Poetry Review, Overland, Portside Review, Proverse Hong Kong, r.kv.r.y quarterly literary journal, Santa Fe Writers Project, Scum Mag, The Suburban Review, Thin Air Magazine* (Northern Arizona University), *Verity La, Visible Ink,* 聲韻詩刊 *Voice & Verse Poetry Magazine*, and *Westerly*. An earlier version of 'imagined nation' was awarded Overland's Fair Australia Prize for Poetry 2017. 'public health the silence of god' placed third in The Fellowship of Australian Writers Western Australia's Tom Collins Poetry Prize 2021.

I wish to thank Fremantle Press and Georgia Richter for taking on this collection and believing so strongly in the work, and Tracy Ryan, who as an editor and a poet brings such care, attention, and support to every interaction. I want to highlight and thank the *Westerly* Writers' Development Program, particularly Catherine Noske and Jo Taylor, as well as the ray of light that is Lucy Dougan; and the network of activity radiating from the Centre for Stories, which contributes so much to the literary ecology of Boorloo. A huge thank you to Ng Yi-Sheng, Stephanie Chan and Janelle Koh for their considered reading of a number of the poems in this collection, and the generous conversations and feedback that ensued. To Edith Podesta, Koh Wan Ching, Stefanos Rassios, Lian Sutton, Sharda Harrison, Mez and Hannah and many, many others – who were there, and who persist with me. And to my immediate family, and to the friends and community who have surrounded and inspired me through the writing of so many of these poems and the work on this collection, and who have generally just been the best: a list which includes Maddie Godfrey, Joe Lui, Sam Nerida, Michelle Aitken, Vidya Rajan, Melanie Julien-Martial, Jess Nyanda Moyle, Grace Chow, Alexa Taylor, Julian Hobba and Jay Anderson.

First published 2022 by
FREMANTLE PRESS

Reprinted 2023.

Fremantle Press Inc. trading as Fremantle Press
PO Box 158, North Fremantle, Western Australia, 6159
fremantlepress.com.au

Cover image illustration and design Holly Dunn, hollydunndesign.com
Printed and bound in Australia by Griffin Press.

A catalogue record for this book is available from the National Library of Australia

ISBN 9781760991319 (paperback)
ISBN 9781760991326 (ebook)

Fremantle Press is supported by the State Government through the Department of Local Government, Sport and Cultural Industries.

Fremantle Press respectfully acknowledges the Wadjak people of the Noongar nation as the traditional owners and custodians of the land where we work in Walyalap.